- 3
- HOLE
- PRESS

First printing
ISBN: 978-0-9982763-7-3

Printed in the USA on recycled paper.
Distributed by Small Press Distribution.
Design by Omnivore.
Edited by Rachel Kauder Nalebuff, Mary Marge Locker,
and Olivia Kan-Sperling.
Copyedited by Mindi Englart.

We gratefully acknowledge the many friends of the Press
who supported this publication.

3 Hole Press
Brooklyn NY
3holepress.org

Cooking As Though You Might Cook Again

Danny Licht
Photographs by Laura Letinsky

But really, Socrates,
what do you suppose all this amounts to?
As I said a little while ago,
it is mere scrapings and shavings of discourse,
cut up into little bits...

Plato

Contents

I.

AGAINST RECIPES

To cook or not to cook: it is a new question in history. In the age of supermarket buffets and liquid meal replacements, cooking at home has never made less sense. Cooking has become a luxury on the one hand and a chore on the other, and it is both of these too much, and it is neither one quite enough, and it has made me wonder, against the odds, against reason, and against common sense: what exactly is cooking for?

I sense that something has been lost within our super-abundance of recipes. It is easy today to find a recipe for anything imaginable or unimaginable online. There are recipes for holiday meals and for picnics, for setting up and for cleaning up, for splitting up cooking and cleaning duties and for waking up rested, for maximizing the work week and for maximizing one's career, for finding love and for sustaining it, for walking alone and for being still, for listening to music and for reading a book. It is a wonderful thing, all of this available wisdom, but I wonder if it is somehow too wonderful, which is to say daunting.

I wonder if this widespread availability of detailed instruction discourages home cooks from thinking about what they are doing while they are doing it. It is an amazing thing that one can now be considered a great cook without actually knowing how to cook anything at all. I wonder if the discouragement from thinking while cooking, from using our senses as much as we use our timers and measuring cups, is making us miserable in the kitchen, anxious to finish, and ultimately happier to have dinner from a box.

I imagine an old way of cooking: an Italian grandmother in her kitchen with the confidence to cook what she pleases. After having spent a long time in the kitchen, this grandmother knows that it does not matter all that much whether she uses two cloves of garlic or six or even ten in her well-loved tomato sauce. So long as the garlic gets cooked, and so long as the dish is seasoned well, the amount of garlic only changes the amount of garlic. The dish will not become better or worse, only more or less garlicky. I imagine a grandmother leaning in to her children and grandchildren to tell them, to promise them, to swear: *It will be delicious, do not worry.*

I will be your grandma. All you need to cook well is a little faith in your own taste, which is to say you must use it, and often. I hope that this book will not pull you by a string and make you cook, for example, a pot of beans, but that it might encourage you to do so by showing you what makes cooking beans such a reasonable thing to do and so worthwhile. I hope it might encourage you to look at the beans, to think about them seriously, and to consider your future together, perhaps for the first time. I do not want to present you with directives only, but also with principles, questions, and considerations. I have found in Italian cuisine a way of cooking continuously, of allowing one thing to lead to another, of open-endedness and casual possibility, and so that is the kind of cooking that follows. But this way of cooking, open-endedly, is hardly regional. There will always be uncertainty in cooking, and this must be accepted and even loved. Things will not go as planned; this is a good thing.

When I read recipes, I hear notes on an idea waiting to come alive. I leave my cookbooks in my bedroom. I hope this book will help you to do the same. Cooking does not need to be a race to the table, and it does not need to have an upper limit on what is possible or what is delicious or even what is beautiful. Instead, it can be a drama in parts, each act vital, and each giving way to the next. It can be like life itself. I hope you will agree.

II.

A POT OF BEANS

Cooking for me often begins in the pantry, where I find beans. I like beans and regret that they are not given a chance by so many. They are too humble to be seen, too small for common fantasy. It should not be this way. Beans are nutritious, delicious, versatile, and cheap, glamorous in their little way. I am at peace when I know I have a pot of beans in the fridge, ready to make into lunch.

When I cook beans, I cook too many. I do this on purpose. I start with a pound of dried beans—cannellini, navy, kidney, or cranberry, though every bean has its appeal. I sort through them for small stones and soak them in water, covered by a few inches, overnight. A pound of beans will make more than four servings and fewer than ten. I like this kind of ambiguity in cooking. It pushes me to keep an open mind, and to err on the side of excess. I like excess in cooking because I like dealing with the consequences.

Soaking the beans in advance of cooking is not strictly necessary, but I have found that doing so makes them more easily digestible, in addition to decreasing their cooking time. When I don't have the foresight, I boil the beans for a few minutes, and then remove the pot from the heat, cover it with a lid, and let the beans sit in the hot water for an hour.

After the beans have soaked, I drain them in a colander, return them to the pot, and cover them again with a few inches of fresh water. This is the liquid they will cook in, and so it should be made flavorful. An onion halved and added to the pot is good, and so are whole peeled cloves of garlic. I like to add a halved jalapeno or a seeded dried chili, bay leaves, and whatever herbs I have on hand; rosemary, thyme, and sage are all good. Lately I have particularly liked using a handful of mint. The important thing to keep in mind when filling the pot is that the beans will taste good regardless of what else goes in, even with nothing added, so long as they are cooked through and seasoned with salt at the end of cooking; salting too early prevents their softening. I add to the pot whatever is around and sounds good. I bring the pot to a boil, reduce it to a simmer, and stir it occasionally.

Probably you will want to know how long the beans will take to cook. It is a normal, obvious question yet difficult to answer directly. The truth is that I don't really know how long anything takes to cook. No one does, and no recipe can tell you. Given that the production of the earth is variable, and so are ovens and so are stoves, not to mention the tastes of individuals, any cooking time is always a suggested cooking time. I can tell you that soaked dried beans take about an hour to cook, but they can take anywhere from half an hour to two hours depending on the age of the beans, the qualities of the water, the intensity of the flame, and so on. In the end, the only relevant rule here is that things should be cooked until they are done.

After half an hour of cooking, try a bean and decide for yourself if it is done. When I started cooking Italian food, I assumed that everything was meant to be cooked until it still had a bite, like pasta. Then I went to Italy and learned that Italians tend to cook vegetables until they are very soft. This surprised and challenged me. I had taken *al dente* to be a rule for all things; I should have known better. At the time, this discovery disoriented me, but I have since come to embrace the tenderness of Italian cooking. Like much else, it is just a preference, and partly a gastrointestinal one, but I like to cook beans until they are very soft yet still composed.

Dried beans
Garlic
Bay leaf
Dried chili
Fresh herbs

III.
WHAT TASTES GOOD

At this point, the beans will not taste good; they will not taste like anything, really, except tap water. This is because we have withheld the salt. Without salt, things taste of nothing; with salt, they begin to taste of what they are. The depth of the bean broth comes through; garlicky flavors emerge, rosemary, the hint of the bay leaf. Something beautiful happens so simply. With more salt, things taste better and better until they just taste like salt. This is a fine line and tempting, so be aware of it and taste often. Some say that using a lot of salt is unhealthy, while others say that it is healthy. I say it is delicious and therefore required. My delusion is that beautiful things are generally true, and I think it is beautiful to imagine that food that tastes good and feels good is good for the body. Only time will tell, but I have faith in the good. For a pound of beans, I use at least a few spoonfuls of salt, let it dissolve, then taste and adjust. If it does not taste good, it does not have enough salt. I usually go on to make something with the beans immediately. When I don't, I refrigerate the beans with their cooking liquid and aromatics together.

Cooking As Though You Might Cook Again

IV.
MAKING PASTA

The first thing I want to do when I have a pot of beans
is make pasta. Pasta with beans is a complete meal.
It is textured and delicious. I used to call this *pasta e fagioli*
until I ordered that at a restaurant and learned that *pasta
e fagioli* is a thin red soup. The dish that follows is not a soup,
and I prefer it, whatever it may be called.

When it comes to choosing a shape of pasta, there are certain
traditional guidelines, which have to do with the marriage
of pasta and sauce. For this one, I like to use *orecchiette,*
"little ears." As the beans and pasta come together, the beans
slip into the ears and are held there safely. This marriage is
about holding, comfort, and listening.

Pasta sauce can be made of very little, almost nothing.
Sliced, fried garlic with chili flakes and pasta water makes
a good sauce. So does olive oil alone, a drizzle in the bowl.
Beef shoulder braised for hours in crushed tomatoes
makes a good sauce, and so do beans. A pasta dish could
be, simply, pasta stirred into beans. And that is what this
one is, more or less.

I am not one to say things like *the chili flakes are optional.*
This is because they are of course optional. Even the onions
are optional; they could be replaced with shallots, garlic,
scallions, or nothing, as taste or supply demands. As you

cook with and without chilis and with or without onions, you will learn what is lost and what is gained by simplification and complication both. Everything in cooking is optional, including the cooking itself. Cookbooks are just books, which are just ideas.

When I make quick pastas such as this one, I begin by boiling the water. Once the sauce is ready, I do not like to wait long for the water to boil. The water may come to a boil too early, but it will stay hot beneath a lid as it waits for its cue. Pasta water, like most cooking water, should be very salty. It is common in kitchens to hear chefs say it should be "salty like the sea." Very little of this salt will be absorbed by the pasta, and yet I should caution you that pasta water can actually be too salty, saltier than the sea, and thereby diminish the pleasure of eating it, which should not be short of enormous.

I like to dice an onion and cook it, along with a bay leaf and a pinch of salt, with enough olive oil to coat the onions in a medium pan over medium heat, stirring often to prevent browning and burning. Beginning with salt helps to extract moisture from the onion, which in turn helps the onion cook evenly. Once the onion is nearly cooked through and oftened, after five or ten minutes, I add a few thinly sliced cloves of garlic, a pinch of chili flakes, and a finely chopped sprig of rosemary leaves. This should cook for a couple of minutes, until the garlic has cooked through and the rosemary becomes fragrant.

You will notice that I have been casual with quantities. I will continue to be as long as I can. Quantities are just proportions, and the importance of proportions in cooking is too often overstated. There are rules of thumb, which are good to keep in mind, and there is hunger and there is satiation. But what matters most is attention to the task at hand, learning from experience, enjoying what you have, and trying again tomorrow. When wondering how much pasta to make, one should wonder how much pasta one wants to eat, wants to serve, and wants to save. What bowl will you be using? Will the meal be of pasta alone? What does 4-6 servings mean anyway? Take the serving bowl and fill it with pasta. The pasta will expand as it cooks and gets sauced, but it will not expand very much. Here is a rule of thumb: make the amount you want to eat.

Once the onions and garlic are cooked through, I add the beans with some of the broth that they made as they cooked. How many beans should you add? About a cup per serving, but more works and less works. Any proportion will be fine, but something amazing happens as the bean-to-pasta ratio approaches one-to-one. The look is unusual, almost edgy, and it makes my mouth water. It is sumptuous, voluptuous. Neither pasta with beans nor beans with pasta, it floats in perfect tension; it is a ratio worth seeking. I cook the mixture for a minute or two, stirring the pan and shaking it gently to emulsify the oil of the onions with the broth of the beans.

Meanwhile, in the pot of salted water, I cook the pasta until it is just underdone, not only *al dente* but even slightly crunchy; the pasta will cook further when it joins the sauce. At this point, I drain the pasta and add it to the sauce and fold the sauce over and into the pasta with a large spoon, from the bottom of the pan to the top, until the sauce and pasta are one. I continue folding gently until the pasta is cooked and the sauce looks saucy and glossy. If it looks dry or grainy, I add another half-cup of bean broth or water. Then I taste it again for salt.

Finally, off the heat, I finish it with finely chopped parsley and a lot of black pepper, and I stir it one more time. I like to serve pasta in pasta bowls, which are midway between a plate and a bowl, shallow enough to expose the pasta to light, but deep enough to keep it warm. They are made for the job they perform, which is to say they are elegant.

I like to serve it with a small bowl of freshly grated parmesan and a bottle of chili oil.

Olive oil
Onion
Bay leaf
Garlic
Rosemary
Cooked beans
Chili flakes
Orecchiette
Parsley
Black pepper
Parmesan
Chili oil

V.

NOTES ON GARNISH

Garnish is said to be superficial—is that such a bad thing?
The purpose of a garnish is to make the dish it joins more
beautiful. More beautiful means here: more balanced,
more dynamic. Even just the process of wondering about
garnish can help the cook to see the almost finished dish
in a new light. What do we have here? What could make it
better? A bland-looking white pasta—say, with beans—
would do well to find some texture and beauty from chopped
parsley or Aleppo pepper or even sesame chili oil. The idea
of garnish encompasses herbs, grated cheeses, seeds and
spices, hot sauce, salsas, sea salt, drizzled olive oil, leftover
vinaigrettes, pickled onions, sliced avocado, and much else.
The pursuit of the right garnish is about looking for contrast,
light with heavy, acidic with oily, fresh with cooked, salty
with sweet. But even attention to the surface alone can be
helpful: where there is much green, in a pesto, for example,
imagine including something red, like sun-dried tomatoes.
Garnish is a final intervention, and it begins by looking at
what lies before you, and asking yourself what could
make it more beautiful, because that is what will make it
more delicious.

VI

WHAT SOUP IS

I want to think about cooking more so that I can think about it less. I like cooking, but I don't like it as much as walking to the park or sitting down. On the other hand, I care about what I eat. I want the food I eat to be good for me and to feel good in me, to taste good, to be reasonably inexpensive, and I want to come by it more or less ethically. In that order, actually. It is lucky that these things do not need to be at odds with each other.

One way to begin cooking, the best way I know, is to begin with what you have. That's what soup is. In Tuscany, there is a famous soup called "Tuscan soup," which is not really a soup so much as a way of using leftovers. When I have beans in the fridge, I make bean soup for lunch.

Soup begins by softening an onion in oil and salt, then adding a few cloves of garlic, chili flakes, and finely chopped herbs. Once the onion is cooked through and the garlic is too, I add any other vegetables I have around. Soup can be an exercise in attention and a tool of economy. What is available, and what sounds good? That will be the soup of the day. Today I had some small zucchini, which I sliced in rounds and cooked for a minute with garlic and oil. Cherry tomatoes, halved, would have made a good addition, and so would broccoli, cauliflower, winter squash, spicy sausage, leftover rice—anything, really. And yet beans, onion, and garlic alone make a good soup, particularly with a sprig of rosemary and a slice of toasted bread.

The additions to the onions should be, one, cooked through, and two, cut small enough to fit on a spoon. If they are not already cooked, they should get cooked with the oil. If they are already cooked (leftover potatoes, for example), they should be cut into appropriately sized pieces, if necessary, and only warmed in the oil for a few seconds before moving on to the next step. Cooking is about knowing what to add and when to add it. The way to learn this—how to cook—is through attention and repetition.

Once the base of the soup has been composed, I add the beans with enough of their cooking liquid for the soup to be soupy, bring the soup to a simmer, simmer for a few minutes so that the flavors come together, and then eat it. Soup is good and hearty this way, rustic and rich, but I often want to garnish it with something fresh, spicy, and garlicky, like green sauce.

Onion
Garlic
Vegetables
Beans
Green sauce

VII.
GREEN SAUCE

My desires are marked by ambivalence. When there are good reasons to do one thing, there are often even better reasons to do something else. Because of this, I try to find encouragement from what is around, to pursue what comes to mind and to trust that things will work out. I go to the store and get what looks good so that I can surround myself in the kitchen with good options only. This way my ambivalence is absorbed by what I have on hand, which remakes it into intuition. When I know I have produce in the house, I do not think in advance about what I will make for dinner. I have learned to trust myself enough to know that what I make will taste good, and that even if it does not, I can always make pasta or have tuna from a can.

I stock up on herbs without thinking too much about it, and so I usually have some in the fridge that are about to go bad. From them I make green sauce. Like pasta, like soup, green sauce can be a container for things unused, a site of reincorporation. I like to begin the sauce with a clove of garlic, pounded in a mortar with salt, or blended in a blender, also with salt. If pounded, the garlic should then be added to the blender with a spoonful of sherry vinegar or lemon juice and a cup or two of herbs, roughly chopped. Any combination of herbs is good, really, but one particularly good combination is parsley, tarragon, and dill. Mint, cilantro, and serrano chili, stemmed and seeded, is also good;

Cooking As Though You Might Cook Again

so is cilantro alone. Mint, basil, tarragon, chives, and any other tender herb can be added to the sauce so long as at least half of the herbs are parsley or cilantro. I then add olive oil, in a stream, until the sauce becomes saucy.

As with anything, the elements of the sauce become the criteria for judging it, for noticing what it is and how to improve it. It is important to taste the sauce and wonder about it. Does it need more salt, more vinegar, more oil? Where will this sauce be used? When making Mexican food, I like to use cilantro, chilis, and lime in the green sauce, but for bean soup I prefer tarragon, dill, and sherry vinegar. When the sauce tastes good, I stir it into a soup or spoon it over chicken.

Garlic
Tender herbs
Vinegar
Fresh chili
Olive oil

VIII.
ROAST CHICKEN

When I have green sauce on hand, I am reminded to roast
chicken. Roast chicken is one of the most beautiful things
I know. You only need a few things to make the best chicken
of your life: a good bird, salt, and two days. There are of
course other ways to make roast chicken, with less time or
with jumbo birds, but I prefer making it this way or
otherwise making something else.

Good chickens come from good butchers, but they are not
always very expensive. I get my chickens from a place called
Marconda's Puritan Poultry on West 3rd Street in Los Angeles,
where the chicken, even in its raw state, is so beautiful,
fresh, and delicious-looking, and so expertly butchered, that
I have a hard time not buying more than I know what I
will do with. Their birds are vegetarian-fed, without growth
hormones, raised locally, and are markedly less expensive
than supermarket birds, which never taste as good. I suggest
you find a good butcher and get acquainted.

I begin with a small bird, 3 to 4 pounds, and season it with
salt and pepper. Seasoning it somewhat heavily is helpful for
making the chicken particularly delicious. It's hard to explain
how much salt to use here, in part because there is no tasting
until it is done, but think about a sugar donut, evenly coated
in sugar; you will want the salt to be about three-fourths as
densely dusted as that, and you will want it evenly seasoned.

Cooking As Though You Might Cook Again

The amount of pepper does not matter too much. I like the taste of black pepper on chicken, and so I use quite a bit. After seasoning, I make space between the skin and the breasts using my finger, and insert a sprig of rosemary or thyme. Then I flip it over and do the same with the two legs. Depending on the day, I might use different herbs like oregano or sage, or nothing. The chicken is no less delicious.

I leave the seasoned chicken in the fridge, uncovered, for two days and two nights. In this time, the salt that first coated the skin will find its way into the flesh and season the chicken throughout. At the same time, the skin will begin to dry out, which will help it to crisp up in the oven.

You will notice that I don't use any oil or butter on this chicken. I learned to cook it this way from *The Zuni Cafe Cookbook*, which notes that chickens have enough fat in them to get the skin crispy, though I will add that a drop of oil in the pan does help prevent the skin from sticking. The simplicity of this technique spoke to me when I first read it and it still speaks to me now: the chicken is good enough as it is.

An hour before it is time to cook the chicken, I take it out of the fridge to bring it closer to room temperature, heat the oven to 475 degrees, and put a cast iron skillet in the middle of the oven to get it hot. It's a good idea to dry the skin of the chicken further with paper towels, particularly the bottom. When it is time to cook, I then place the bird in the hot pan using tongs, and cook it like that for 30 minutes. If the oven gets very smoky, I lower the temperature to 450 degrees and remember to clean it later. After half an hour, I use a spatula to loosen any stuck skin, and then with tongs flip it upside down, and cook it for 10-15 minutes more. Finally, I flip it back right-side up for another 10 minutes or so.

When is the chicken done? This is an important question for food safety reasons. When is the chicken overdone? This is an important question for the sake of succulence. One way to find out is to stick a thermometer into the thickest part of the chicken leg, and to see that it has reached at least 165 degrees Fahrenheit. I find this method very confusing. I can never seem to find the thickest part of the leg, and so I can never seem to get an accurate or useful reading. Instead, after 45 minutes of baking, I make an incision where the leg meets the body. If the juices run clear, I know the chicken is done. If it is not, I wait another five or ten minutes and check the other leg. When the juices run clear, and the leg rather easily pulls away, the chicken is done; I take it out right away. The chicken will cook further, slightly, as it rests. This method has worked for me consistently, with my chickens and the ovens that I have used.

A chicken should rest for at least 15 minutes before carving because its juices, when hot, run out of the chicken and leave it drier than it would be otherwise. As the chicken mellows and cools off from the heat, the juices mellow too. They relax and join the flesh, and they leave the chicken tasting extremely delicious. Carving a chicken can seem challenging at first, but it is actually very easy with a little practice and a sharp knife. I suggest watching a few YouTube videos to help.

I like to serve the chicken with green sauce, crispy potatoes, boiled broccoli, and a simple salad.

Small chicken
Salt and pepper
Rosemary or thyme
Green sauce

IX

POTATOES

It is easy to cook potatoes. I cut them into pieces the size
I want to eat them, toss them in a bowl with enough olive
oil to make them shine, a bay leaf, garlic cloves, chili flakes,
sprigs of rosemary or thyme, pepper, and enough salt to
make them taste good. I toss the potatoes with my hands,
then taste one; the salt should be prominent. Then I line
a sheet tray with parchment paper and dump the potatoes
onto it. Sometimes I make sure the potatoes are all cut-
side down to ensure they get crispy. I cook them in a hot
oven, around 400 degrees, until they are cooked through
and easy to cut with the side of a fork, 20 or 30 minutes,
depending on the size and type of potato and the heat of the
oven. Sometimes I gently move the potatoes around after
15 minutes, or rotate the pan.

Potatoes
Olive oil
Bay leaf
Garlic
Chili flakes
Rosemary

X.

SALAD

For a long time I have been confused by the way we talk
about food in this country. Before I found an interest in food
and cooking, I assumed that so-called organic food had
to be some kind of scam, given that, in a certain sense of
the word, every plant and animal fits the category easily.
But as I learned more about the industrial farming practices
developed in the last century, something like the reverse
began to seem true. I was haunted by the fact that the apples
I ate were grown with the help of synthetic chemical
pesticides, and that the meat I ate came from cows raised
on a diet of grain laced with antibiotics. It became clear to
me that the produce without a name, the mere "apples"
sitting beside the "organic apples," should be the kind with
the special designation.

Our vocabulary in the kitchen has been co-opted by the
marketing departments of food-processing and agrochemical
conglomerates. Freeze-dried mashed potatoes are now
called "homestyle," while actual potatoes, fresh from the
market, boiled with salt and served unadorned, are considered
gourmet, even fussy. Ranch dressing, with its hundred
ingredients, is simple fare, while a vinaigrette, with its three,
is fancy. A good, simple salad with fresh greens and a light
dressing could hardly be easier to make, and every meal is
improved by its being there. Making such a salad can be a
small resistance to the upside-down marketing language of

the times we live in. In other words, it seems to me a central lesson of good cooking.

I tend to dress salads with vinaigrettes, because there is almost nothing better. I begin with red wine vinegar— a couple of teaspoons, say, which I mix with a pinch of salt. People often imagine a pinch to mean something like six or seven granules, but I never mean less than a teaspoon. I whisk these together until the salt dissolves into the vinegar, because salt does not dissolve as easily in oil. I then slowly whisk in good olive oil, maybe a few tablespoons, then taste it, and add more vinegar, more olive oil, and more salt until it is to my liking. That's it. It is a delicious salad dressing as is, but it can be modified in several exciting ways.

Adding to a vinaigrette begins by adding to the vinegar. A finely diced or thinly sliced shallot is a good addition, so is a pounded or finely grated clove of garlic. A few pounded anchovy fillets make a good vinaigrette incredibly delicious. A spoonful of mustard can be a good addition, as can chopped dill, orange zest, or sherry vinegar, which might replace some or all of the red wine vinegar. What is important to pay attention to, as always, is what sounds good to you and what will be appropriate for the given meal. With a very heavy meal, like a rich, meaty pasta, I want an especially acidic salad with a lot of coarsely chopped parsley and dill tossed in at the end. With lighter meals, the salad can be more composed and complex. A plate of beans and rice warmly welcomes thinly sliced radishes, cilantro, and pickled red onions. At times balance means light with heavy, bright with rich, and at other times it means potent with potent. Anchovies and garlic in a dressing—the most delicious combination I know—is especially strong and

could go equally well with a white fish, a roast chicken,
or a ribeye steak.

What is good and right to cook at any given moment depends
on the season and the availability of things, and above all on
the desire of the cook. What I like about cooking is that it is a
way of seeing, holding, and pursuing my immediate interests.
Cooking is pleasurable for me only insofar as I can cook
what I want to cook, but what I want is fragile, elusive, and
changes depending on what is around. Every time I cook, I
have a better sense of what I want, what I like, and how I can
achieve it. To be hungry for what can be had: that is the idea.

I dress salads with a little dressing at a time, and I toss them
with my hands, trying to coat every green. I taste a leaf
and add some salt, or some vinegar, or some oil, and serve it
on a chilled plate.

Red wine vinegar
Olive oil
Salad greens

Cooking As Though You Might Cook Again

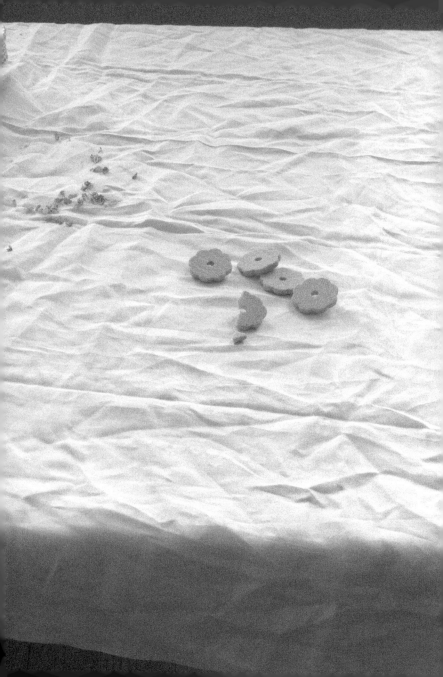

XI.

USING THE BONES

A chicken died for you; make the most of its life by making
stock from its bones. It is easy to do. Chicken stock can be
this alone: chicken boiled in water. I put the roasted carcass,
meat removed, in a pot and fill it to the top with water, bring
the water to a boil, reduce it to a simmer, cook it for as much
time as I am willing to give it, and then strain it when it is
done. I never care that much whether the stock is strong or
mild, so I don't worry too much about how long it cooks.
Two hours is a good amount of time, but anywhere from
one to four hours works. I like to add a tablespoon or so of
apple cider vinegar, which helps break down the bones.
Aromatics are good too: a head of garlic halved along its
equator, a quartered onion, a few bay leaves, parsley stems,
rosemary or thyme. If the stock will be had on its own,
as in a chicken soup, then it is more important to include
aromatics. But even in a dish where the stock will be
just another ingredient, like in a risotto or a braise, I do
believe that the flavors, aromas, and oils of delicious
things added help to provide an unnameable complexity
that I will dare to call a soul.

Chicken bones
Apple cider vinegar
Onion
Herb stems
Bay leaves

Cooking As Though You Might Cook Again

XII.
MAKING RISOTTO

Risotto is another dish that can be made easily and without
hand-holding. It is built on a single principle: add more
liquid until it is done. What's more is that it instructs its
cook to look around the kitchen for ideas. It is the kind
of thing I like to make. The liquid base of risotto should be
chicken stock, but it can also be water or vegetable stock.
I always prefer water to shelf-stable boxed stock.

Risotto is a thick, creamy rice dish made without cream.
I have made it vegan on occasion, but I generally prefer
it with parmesan, butter, and chicken stock—what a nice
group of words. I like risotto with peas, mushrooms,
summer squash, winter squash, a piece of fish, broccolini,
and bacon—I mean separately, though peas and bacon
seem suddenly destined for each other. And risotto alone,
cooked plain and well with good parmesan and olive oil,
is a delight in itself.

Every risotto begins the way so many things do, with an
onion. I dice an onion and cook it in olive oil with salt and a
bay leaf over medium heat in a large, wide pan in order to
soften it, avoiding browning it. Once the onion is softened,
I add a few cloves of sliced garlic (my private rule is one clove
per person), and cook for another minute, until the garlic
is cooked through. At this point, I add the rice. My rule of
thumb is two handfuls of dried rice per person; this has

worked well for me. As you cook more and see how much you like to eat, and how much you like to have left, you can adjust that amount.

You will notice that the amount of onion that I suggest (one) remains invariable for an undisclosed number of servings (two to six, let's say). How is this possible? It is possible because it just doesn't matter very much. Everything involved here is delicious. Rice is delicious, onion is delicious, garlic is delicious, broth is delicious. In combination with salt, pepper, and cheese, one simply cannot go wrong. Of course a very serious cook with a very refined palate and a reputation to uphold will want to cook with great consistency and exactness. But I am young and free; I want to eat well and soon, not perfectly.

Moreover, I believe there is virtue in attending to intuition, that intuitive cooking, no matter how it ends up looking, holds some inimitable charm. Dishes plated by experienced, unafraid cooks have a graceful quality that those plated by anxious cooks, even very skilled ones, lack. One way to assuage a fear of cooking is to cling to the word of a recipe; that way, the recipe can be blamed for a mediocre dish as opposed to the cook. In my cooking, I have no interest in blame, and I have no interest in clinging. I am interested only in the things that lie before me and the meal that will follow. Sometimes I fail, but never too badly. It really is hard to fail badly. An onion might burn; I throw it away or embrace it. Or maybe I go too heavy on the salt, so I add more water. Along the way I might discover that a loose, soupy risotto, like a Japanese rice porridge, is even more satisfying than the meal I'd originally planned.

Cooking As Though You Might Cook Again

Let us return to where we were. I like to toast the rice for a few minutes in the cooked onion, garlic, and oil mixture, without liquid. While this happens, I bring the chicken stock to a boil in a separate pot, and then turn off the flame and ready the ladle. Once the rice is toasted (not burnt), I pour in enough wine to nearly submerge it. Dry white wine will yield a respectable, presentable risotto, but red wine is fine, too, and alluring in its own way. In the absence of wine, a few tablespoons of wine vinegar added to the stock will suffice.

Risotto is famously about stirring, and it really does need to be stirred more or less constantly, over medium heat, with particular attention paid to moving the grains of rice at the bottom of the pan. Once the wine is absorbed, I ladle in hot chicken stock until it almost covers the top of the rice, and keep stirring. Once that is absorbed, more stock, and more stirring. Then I add a few big pinches of salt, stir, and add more stock. I taste, adjust the salt, and keep stirring. Once the rice begins to appear saturated and cooked, I taste it again. When it is cooked through but still firm, *al dente* like pasta, I remove it from the heat and stir in more hot stock to thin it slightly, or I use water if I have run out of stock. I finish the risotto with more salt if needed, pepper, a tablespoon or two of butter, and quite a bit of grated parmesan. Lemon zest and juice are good additions, too, to cut through the fattiness.

A big plate of risotto is a gift. Good, thick balsamic vinegar drizzled on top makes it a gift from God. More grated parmesan is good, too—so is fresh arugula, and of course the rest of the bottle of wine.

Olive oil
Onion
Bay leaf
Garlic
Wine
Chicken stock
Short-grain rice
Butter
Parmesan
Lemon

XIII.
FRIED RISOTTO

Cold risotto is good, if sad. Fried risotto is miles better, if heavy. I like to eat only a small amount of this, but I like it so much that I find it is worth the small effort. When I have risotto leftover, I roll it into small balls or discs, roll these in flour with salt, then into a couple of whisked eggs, then coat them in breadcrumbs mixed with salt, and then finally fry them in a half-inch of olive oil until they turn deeply golden. Then I flip them to brown the other side. It is easy enough to do and extremely delicious, particularly with a sharp, bright arugula salad.

Risotto
Flour
Egg
Breadcrumbs
Olive oil

XIV.

MAYONNAISE

What makes fried risotto even better, even insanely good,
is mayonnaise. Mayonnaise makes many things better.
From a jar it is delicious, but made fresh it is decidedly
transcendent. The everyday condiment becomes something
worth coveting. It is surprisingly easy to make, too.

It begins with an egg yolk in a heavy bowl. I whisk it
with a pinch of salt and with or without a clove or two
of pounded garlic until it thickens slightly. With garlic,
mayonnaise becomes aioli. At this point I measure
out half a cup of canola oil and half a cup of olive oil into
a measuring cup with a spout, and pour one single drop
of oil into the yolk and mix it in. It is so important to begin
slowly. With the addition of too much oil at the beginning,
the mayonnaise will never emulsify and it will be horrible.
Failed, broken mayos have left me feeling impotent and
despondent, confused and irritable. I wish I were joking.
After some early success making mayonnaise, I became
overconfident. I did not believe the rules applied to me. I did
not think that moving slowly, drop by drop, could actually
make a difference in the end. How wrong I was!

Now I am confident in making mayonnaise but in a
different way. I am confident in my gentleness, my patience,
my insistence on the drop-by-drop. After the first drop
is combined with the yolk, I drop in another, and then,

when that is combined, another, then another. After half the oil is combined in this way, I am free to pour more quickly, whisking all the while, but still and always in a slow, steady stream. It is amazing to see the mayonnaise get thicker as more oil is added to it.

Some kind of magic is occurring; it is called mayonnaise. Once all the oil is mixed in, I squeeze in a few drops of lemon juice or a teaspoon of vinegar, taste it, and maybe add some more salt or more lemon. If it is too thick but acidic enough, I whisk in a little water until it is satisfyingly viscous and ploppy.

Egg yolk
Salt
Garlic
Canola oil
Olive oil
Lemon

XV.
SALMON WITH MAYO

Whatever sauce I make, I always have some left over, and
when I have mayonnaise left over, I want to eat it with fish.
I first heard about eating salmon with aioli in a book by
Alice Waters. As a Jew, the thought of eating fish with mayo
was foreign to me, but it was at the same time immediately,
hauntingly alluring. Something about the texture of
salmon and its subtle, meaty flavor, even just in my mind,
came together with the salty, fatty, gooey qualities of garlicky
mayonnaise. Recently I have been cooking salmon the
following way and eating it with mayo, and, since I first did,
I have not cooked it any other way.

When I have many herbs in the fridge, I often think of fish.
I begin with a fillet of salmon, about half a pound per person.
In a pan that can comfortably yet cozily fit the whole fillet,
I lay a bed of herbs for the fish. Dill, parsley, and cilantro all
work very well, as do the green stems of fennel and rings
of lemon. These will not flavor the fish so much as perfume
it. I then lay the salmon, skin side down, on top of the herbs,
and season it rather generously with salt and rather less
generously with chili powder. Then I douse the whole thing
with olive oil, so that it is glazed with the oil, and so that the
herb bed is too. Sometimes I rub in the chili and salt, gently,
with my fingers, in order to achieve a more even seasoning.
I let this sit out at room temperature for 15 minutes to allow
the seasoning to settle into the flesh and then bake the

salmon at 400 degrees for 15 or 20 minutes, until the white
fat of the salmon begins to rise to the top. When this
first happens, it indicates that the salmon has just cooked
through, cooked about medium or medium-rare, how
I like it. If you like it cooked more thoroughly, I suggest
cooking it more thoroughly. Actually, I don't really, but
I can't exactly stop you.

Once the salmon is cooked and removed from the oven,
I use a big spoon to carve out rough servings of the fish;
the skin should easily separate from the flesh. I place the
pieces on plates or a platter, then tilt the pan to spoon some
of the pan olive oil, now a sauce, on top of the fish. I serve
it with a spoonful of mayonnaise and boiled broccoli.

Salmon fillet
Salt
Herbs
Olive oil
Mayonnaise

XVI.

BOILED BROCCOLI

Boiling is the easiest way to cook a vegetable, and one of the best, so long as the vegetable is good and fresh. I bring a pot of water to a boil, big enough to fit all the broccoli I want to cook, and season the water heavily with salt. I cut the broccoli to the size I want to eat it, drop it in, and cook it for a few minutes, until it is easy to eat and seasoned throughout with salt. I drain the water and drizzle the broccoli with olive oil. Light, fresh, and salty, I like to serve boiled vegetables with fish especially. Mayonnaise doesn't hurt and neither would a vinaigrette.

Broccoli
Olive oil

Cooking As Though You Might Cook Again

XVII.

FRITTATA

Because it is an egg dish, frittata seems to be for breakfast, but it is equally good for lunch or dinner, especially with a nice little salad and a good bottle of wine. Wine makes it elegant. Frittata is another home for lost foods, a way to make what is leftover fresh, vibrant, and new. This frittata is made with broccoli in mind, but any vegetable, leftover or not, will work, some better than others. Cooked carrots are good, and potatoes are traditional. Eggplant would be bizarre, but I would be open to trying it. Well, now I am imagining an eggplant frittata served with a spoonful of tomato sauce, grated ricotta salata, and chopped mint. Clearly that is a good idea.

It is helpful to have a nonstick pan for this. I like to use a small one, eight inches or so in diameter, for a frittata that will serve two or three people, depending on hunger. I heat up the pan and warm the leftover broccoli in it with some olive oil. While the broccoli is heating up, I whisk eggs, four to six, in a bowl until they are largely homogenized. More eggs will yield a thicker, more substantial frittata. I like to play with the ratio of vegetable to egg. The maximum amount of egg is the maximum that will fit in the pan; the minimum is the amount that will hold it all together. The rest is left to the cook's discretion. Try to visualize it as you go. I add the hot vegetable to the whisked eggs with some salt, imagining that I am seasoning each egg individually, in order to get an idea of the appropriate amount of salt. I add more oil to the pan, warm it over medium heat, and pour in the egg mixture. This will cook for several minutes, until the top is just nearly set but still runny. At that point I search for a plate that is just larger than the pan. It is time to flip.

The flip is precarious, fun, dangerous, and rewarding. I run a butter knife around the edge of the frittata to loosen it, place the plate upside down on the pan, and flip the two of them over together, quickly and carefully. Then I add a little more oil to coat the pan, and gently slide the half-cooked frittata back onto the pan. It is a move that requires attention but does not demand much dexterity or skill on the part of the cook. It is actually easy. At this point the frittata is more than half-cooked; it is almost done. I cook it on its second side for just one or two more minutes, until it appears cooked to my liking, and then flip it onto a plate or cutting board to be served, with or without wine.

Cooked vegetables
Olive oil
Eggs

XVIII.

BRAISING MEAT

Leftover wine is not a waste but a gift from one's past to
one's present. It presents an opportunity to deepen the
flavor of a special dish. It brings the complexity of the wine—
rich, acidic dimensions—into the fold of a given meal.
In dishes that have both tomatoes and wine, it is generally
thought that red wine goes best, but I sometimes like white
wine even better; it is lighter, brighter, and seems more
playful. And if it's what you have open, then it's what you
should use.

One of the most delicious things in the world is long-braised
meat. Pork shoulder braised with orange, cumin, carrots,
and beer makes for some of the greatest tacos on earth.
The thought of lamb tagine, with saffron, turmeric, tomato,
and couscous, falling apart beside hot bread and harissa,
gives me chills and inhabits my dreams.

Other nights, I dream of pasta. Once it was rigatoni with
beef, falling apart in a deep, beautiful tomato sauce.
The next morning, I made it a reality. I braised chuck beef
with tomatoes, onion, garlic, and wine, and made it into
a pasta sauce for rigatoni. Pieces of beef slid into the pasta's
tubes, filling some like ravioli. On top, I grated lemon
zest and parmesan, and garnished it with basil. It was a
revelation. It was a knock on heaven's door. I sent a picture
to my friend, who is Italian, and he said, "Genovese?"

The sauce, it turns out, has been around for five hundred years. It remains as delicious as ever, and apparently resides in the collective unconscious.

The first step is to season the meat. I like to make about two pounds of meat per pound of pasta, which serves about four people—though, as usual, making more is a good idea. In addition to a sauce for pasta, braised beef can make for a ridiculously good sandwich, with mustard and pickled onions, as well as a topping for polenta.

I cut the meat into two-inch cubes, season them very generously with salt, and let them sit at room temperature for twenty or thirty minutes. Then I pat the meat dry with a paper towel to help it brown. In a Dutch oven, I heat up enough olive oil to coat the pan, and then add the pieces of meat one by one. Sometimes this has to be done in batches. I brown each side, flipping them over with tongs, until they are browned and crisped all over, and then set them on a plate to wait. Browning meat is a crucial step for building flavor. The crisped up, caramelized edges of beef drastically enrich the dish.

I pour out the beef fat, pour in more olive oil, and cook a couple of diced onions there. If I have a carrot or two and a rib of celery, I add those too, cut into pieces roughly the same size as the onion. I cook these over medium heat with salt and a bay leaf until they are cooked through and browned but not burnt. As they sweat and cook, they will begin to loosen the browned bits of beef stuck to the base of the pan. The rest of these will emerge when I add the wine.

Once the onion is nearly cooked, I add several cloves of garlic, sliced, and cook for another minute. Then I add tomato paste. It is possible, and perhaps advisable, to use a whole tube or jar of tomato paste here. I like tomato paste because its flavor is dense, rich, even, and smooth. It lends tomato flavor without tomato texture, and sometimes that is what I want. There is quite a bit of roughness in braised meat already. I pour in a glass of wine, add a pinch of salt, and stir the mixture, making sure to scrape the bottom of the pan.

I add the meat back to the pot and bring this mixture up to a boil to cook off the alcohol, then down to a simmer, cover it with a lid, and cook it at a low temperature until the meat easily falls apart at the hands of a butter knife, about two hours.

At this point, the pieces of beef may be spooned out and onto a bowl of polenta and served with a salad (I am thinking frisée) for a very good meal. What is left should become pasta.

Chuck beef
Onions
Carrot
Garlic
Tomato
Wine

XIX.
MAKING PASTA II

Braised meat goes with pasta. I don't know what else to tell
you. When I have leftover braised meat in the fridge, it is
like Christmas for pasta. It is like a miracle. Linguini is good,
but I usually want rigatoni, thick ribbed tubes of pasta.
I like the way the pieces of meat sink into it. But every shape
of pasta comes with its own particular pleasures. I heat
up the meat and stir aggressively so that it falls apart. If it
does not, I roughly chop each piece on a cutting board,
and return them to the pot and try again. If the meat was
left in the fridge, it will have thickened up overnight
and so must be loosened. To do that, I add some water.

I cook some pasta. Again, the amount is up to the cook.
It could be a beef stew with some pasta floating around,
or it could be a pasta with meat sauce. I cook the pasta very
al dente, add half a cup of its salty, starchy cooking water
to the meat, and then drain the pasta and add it to the sauce.
I stir it around and pay attention. Do I want it thinner?
I add more water. Is the sauce broken, the oil separated and
greasy-looking? If it is, I keep stirring, and add more
water again. I taste it, and add some salt, pepper, and chili
flakes. I taste it again.

With a big spoon, I plate it into pasta bowls, and I grate
lemon zest and parmesan on top of each plate. Then I douse
each with some good olive oil and call it Genovese.

Cooking As Though You Might Cook Again

Braised meat
Rigatoni
Chili flakes
Lemon zest
Parmesan

XX.
DEVELOPING VARIATION

I am at a loss. Nothing can easily follow rigatoni alla
Genovese. Eating something like that—reasonably complex
and exceedingly delicious—brings me back to what
has become my refrain in cooking, my developing theme,
the humble pot of beans.

The day after having the rigatoni, I might cook some beans
in one pot and some rice in another, with salt, sesame oil,
and a bunch of mint. If I have vegetables in the fridge,
I might cook them with an onion and garlic, stir them into
the beans, and spoon the mixture over rice. I begin cooking
again simply, heartily, easily, almost without having to think.
I am never disappointed by a bowl of beans and rice for
lunch, and I am happy to know that, with the rest of that pot
waiting in the fridge, I will soon be led towards another
meal and further cooking. This is the way I like to cook.

XXI.

LITTLE CHOCOLATE CAKE

Something is missing, and it is dessert. This dark and boozy chocolate cake is the only one I need. I think that it completes the meal.

I have said that I would be as loose as I could with quantities and proportions, but in baking, a certain precision is called for. Imprecise baking can easily result in failures—sad desserts, wasted eggs and chocolate. I don't wish that upon you, or them. And so I present you with numbers, quantities, and measurements, dutifully. This recipe makes five or six hefty servings, and it is easily doubled. I should note that it reheats well.

6 oz bittersweet chocolate (60-67%), chopped
5 tablespoons unsalted butter, plus some for the pan
1/4 cup whiskey
2 eggs, separated
3/4 cup sugar
1/2 cup unbleached all-purpose flour
A pinch of salt

4 oz bittersweet chocolate (60-67%), chopped
1/2 cup heavy cream

Heat the oven to 350 degrees. Butter a seven-inch cake pan and line the base with parchment paper. Boil six ounces of chocolate over a double boiler with the butter and the whiskey. I like to use a glass mixing bowl over a pot of simmering water for this.

In a separate large bowl, whisk the egg yolks with half of the sugar until it thickens; this will take a few minutes. Mix in the melted chocolate mixture, then the flour and salt until they are just combined.

Separately, and preferably with an electric mixer, whisk the egg whites until they are fluffy; then add the rest of the sugar. Once the whites become structured and stiff, after about five minutes, fold the whites into the chocolate, in three parts, until the batter is evenly smooth and combined.

Pour the batter into the cake pan and cook the cake for about 25-30 minutes, until a cracked crust has formed over the center and a knife inserted into the center comes out almost clean.

In another double-boiler, melt four ounces of chocolate with the heavy cream until it is combined and silky and smooth. Run a knife around the edge of the cake, and flip it onto a plate. Then flip it onto another plate so it is upright, and pour the warm, silky chocolate on top. This cake is best served warm, with creme fraiche or ice cream.

What is good in cooking is never secret but always hard to relate. In some meals, the elements seem to align. Unfussy food on a simple table can feel like magic. The truth is that it is not hard to cook well. On the other hand, it does take practice to cook pleasurably. There will be failures in the process, some bad and some worse. But cooking is a project that is both a part of life and a metaphor for it, so it is worth doing thoughtfully. I have come to learn that the magic of a good meal is that there is no magic—just attention, just care. Of course recipes have an important place in cooking. Numbers can be helpful, but they cannot replace the knowledge that comes from being the one who is alive in the kitchen. I like reading recipes to learn about methods and combinations, and then returning to the kitchen refreshed and excited but unencumbered by the preferences of some other cook. I use recipes only insofar as they suit me and what I have on hand. Some of my favorite books are cookbooks and I like reading them before bed. They soothe me, comfort me, console me, and excite me; they give substance to my dreams. Then in the morning, as I sit with my coffee, I get to wondering: what do I really want?

COOKING AS THOUGH YOU MIGHT COOK AGAIN

Cooking should begin with what you have. It is not a radical notion but an ancient one, if forgotten or lost. I avoid saying "using leftovers"—it is too drab. It sounds like a last resort, a chore, a microwave's beep. Let your food become your meal, and let your senses guide your menu. To cook well and forever you need only a handful of techniques and an eye for possibility. Boiling, baking, frying, and braising will take you far if you let them. The seasons change, and variety comes with them, but the way of cooking does not change. Cook things until they are done and season them until they taste good. Everything else is optional and will come in time. The point is to cook casually, to find a way that suits you, and to walk through the market with an open mind, trusting that when you get home, you will be able to make something of whatever it is you have found. Your senses are much wiser than any recipe could be. They are what you have with you, and so they are the place you should begin.

Cooking As Though You Might Cook Again

Artworks by Laura Letinsky © Laura Letinsky

Pages 6–7
Untitled #13, *Hardly More Than Ever* series, 1998.

Pages 8–9
Untitled #20, *The Dog and the Wolf* series, 2010.

Pages 18–19
Untitled #3, *Hardly More Than Ever* series, 1997.

Pages 26–27
Untitled #36, *Hardly More Than Ever* series, 2001.

Pages 36–37
Untitled #9, *Hardly More Than Ever* series, 1997.

Pages 42–43
Untitled #24, *Hardly More Than Ever* series, 1999.

Page 65
Untitled #39, *Hardly More Than Ever* series, 2001.

Pages 68–69
Untitled #55, *Hardly More Than Ever* series, 2002.

Page 71
Untitled #32, *The Dog and the Wolf* series, 2009.

Cooking As Though You Might Cook Again

ACKNOWLEDGMENTS

This book owes much to the vision of Rachel Kauder Nalebuff, who believed that something might come from nothing (so to speak), and so it did. I am grateful to Mary Marge Locker, Alice Chung, and Laura Letinsky for their distinct yet immeasurable contributions to the book, which have made it into something to behold. I learned to cook at Chez Panisse, which might be obvious at this point to anyone else who did. Everyone I met there was a genius, including my fellow interns, and I feel lucky to have learned from them. I am grateful to the local farmers, who make cooking well an easy job, and for the support of my friends and family, especially my parents. This book is dedicated to my mom and my teachers, with thanks and admiration.

Cooking As Though You Might Cook Again